Contents

Any words appearing in the text in bold,
like this, are explained in the Glossary.

Waste issues around the World

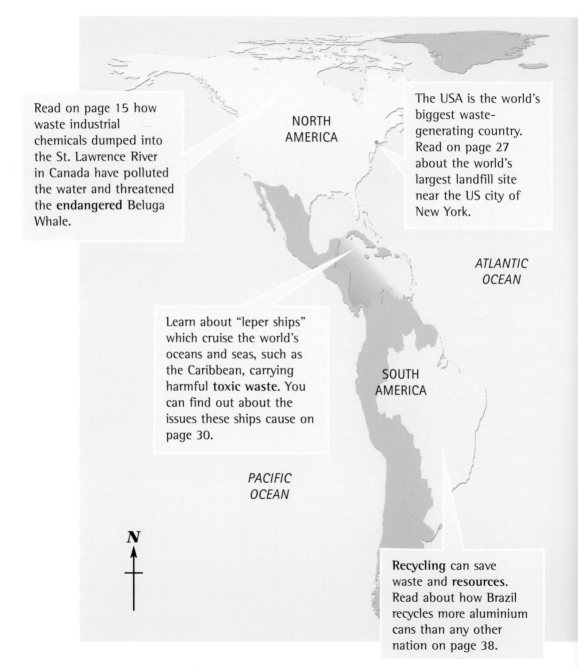

Read on page 15 how waste industrial chemicals dumped into the St. Lawrence River in Canada have polluted the water and threatened the **endangered** Beluga Whale.

NORTH AMERICA

The USA is the world's biggest waste-generating country. Read on page 27 about the world's largest landfill site near the US city of New York.

ATLANTIC OCEAN

Learn about "leper ships" which cruise the world's oceans and seas, such as the Caribbean, carrying harmful **toxic waste**. You can find out about the issues these ships cause on page 30.

SOUTH AMERICA

PACIFIC OCEAN

N

Recycling can save waste and **resources**. Read about how Brazil recycles more aluminium cans than any other nation on page 38.

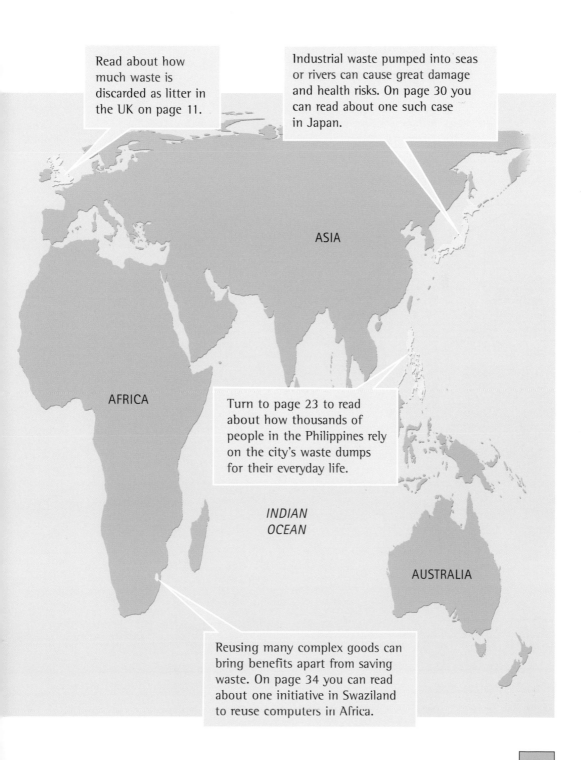

Read about how much waste is discarded as litter in the UK on page 11.

Industrial waste pumped into seas or rivers can cause great damage and health risks. On page 30 you can read about one such case in Japan.

ASIA

AFRICA

Turn to page 23 to read about how thousands of people in the Philippines rely on the city's waste dumps for their everyday life.

INDIAN
OCEAN

AUSTRALIA

Reusing many complex goods can bring benefits apart from saving waste. On page 34 you can read about one initiative in Swaziland to reuse computers in Africa.

A wasteful world?

Waste is something that is thrown away because the person or organization who owns it no longer wants it, cannot use it, or cannot sell it. Waste is sometimes thought of as having no use or value, but it can be useful. For example, a car which no longer runs can be a good source of spare parts, whilst discarded plastics, metals, and paper can all be recycled and made into new materials.

Waste in nature

Nature produces waste when leaves fall from trees, plants and animals die, and living things **excrete** waste into their environment. Any waste substance produced by a living thing is called organic waste – around a fifth of the weight of an average British or American household dustbin is made up of organic waste. Left alone, nature **biodegrades** almost everything it makes back into basic building blocks, so that new living things can be made from the old ones. For example, dead plants rot into the soil providing it with useful **nutrients**. However, not all natural waste is useful or harmless. For instance, some human and animal waste can spread deadly diseases.

Many forms of organic waste are biodegradable. This means that they can be broken down naturally by agents in the environment such as **bacteria**. Non-biodegradable materials, such as glass, do not decay and rot down. Others, such as plastics or some man-made fabrics, do so only over a very long period of time. In the past, nearly all waste created by people was biodegradable. However, today millions of tonnes of non-biodegradable waste are generated.

Landfill sites

Many materials require certain conditions, such as sunlight, water, or the presence of particular bacteria, to biodegrade. Large numbers of products that will biodegrade on the earth's surface, such as food and paper, struggle to biodegrade when buried deep in rubbish dumps, known as landfill sites. The University of Arizona's Tucson Garbage Project studied waste in the past by investigating old landfill sites. There, they discovered newspapers dating back to 1952, and food items which had not biodegraded, including 25-year-old hot dogs and corn cobs!

www.raintreepublishers.co.uk

Visit our website to find out more information about **Raintree** books.

To order:

 Phone 44 (0) 1865 888113

 Send a fax to 44 (0) 1865 314091

 Visit the Raintree bookshop at **www.raintreepublishers.co.uk** to browse our catalogue and order online.

First published in Great Britain by Raintree, Halley Court, Jordan Hill, Oxford OX2 8EJ, part of Harcourt Education.
Raintree is a registered trademark of Harcourt Education Ltd.

Editorial: Sarah Shannon and Louise Galpine
Design: Lucy Owen and Bridge Creative Services Ltd
Picture Research: Natalie Gray and Sally Cole
Production: Chloe Bloom

Originated by Repro Multi Warna
Printed and bound in China by South China Printing Company

ISBN 1 844 43976 3 (hardback)
10 09 08 07 06
10 9 8 7 6 5 4 3 2 1

ISBN 1 844 43983 6 (paperback)
ISBN 978 1 844 43983 6 (paperback)
11 10 09 08 07
11 10 9 8 7 6 5 4 3 2 1

British Library Cataloguing in Publication Data
Gifford, Clive
Waste. – (Planet under pressure)
363.7

A full catalogue record for this book is available from the British Library.

Acknowledgements
The Publishers would like to thank the following for permission to reproduce photographs:
Alamy pp. **10, 42, 44, 46, 48** (Janine Weidel), **17** (Harald Theissen), **40–41** (Michael Klinec); Alamy/SDM Images pp. **36–37**; Alamy/Travelstock pp. **40–41**; Corbis p. **15** (Michael Yamashita), **26** (Roger Wood) **30–31** (Roger Ressmeyer), **34–35** (Philip Corwin); Corbis/Sygma pp. **18** (B. Bisson), **28–29** Jacques Pavlovsky; Digital Vision/Harcourt Education Ltd pp. **8-9, 16, 22–23**; ENCAMS pp. **10–11**; Greenpeace **30–31**; Panos p. **14** (G. M. B. Akash), **34–35** (Giacomo Pirozzi); Still Pictures pp. **4–5, 6–7** (David Drain), **18–19** (William Campbell), **24** (Jonathan Kaplan), **26–27** (Mark Edwards), **32–33** (Martin Bond), **38–39** (David Woodfall); Trip pp. **12–13** (M. Barlow).

Cover photographs of rubbish dump reproduced with kind permission of Corbis, and of sewage plant reproduced with kind permission of Getty.

Every effort has been made to contact copyright holders of any material reproduced in this book. Any omissions will be rectified in subsequent printings if notice is given to the publishers.

Dedicated to the memory of Lucy Owen

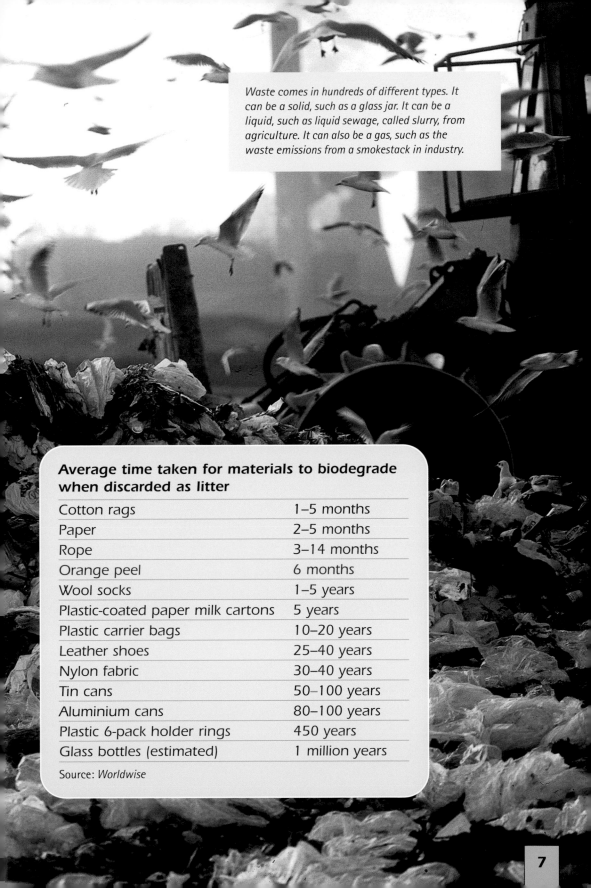

Waste comes in hundreds of different types. It can be a solid, such as a glass jar. It can be a liquid, such as liquid sewage, called slurry, from agriculture. It can also be a gas, such as the waste emissions from a smokestack in industry.

Average time taken for materials to biodegrade when discarded as litter

Cotton rags	1–5 months
Paper	2–5 months
Rope	3–14 months
Orange peel	6 months
Wool socks	1–5 years
Plastic-coated paper milk cartons	5 years
Plastic carrier bags	10–20 years
Leather shoes	25–40 years
Nylon fabric	30–40 years
Tin cans	50–100 years
Aluminium cans	80–100 years
Plastic 6-pack holder rings	450 years
Glass bottles (estimated)	1 million years

Source: *Worldwise*

Top ten generators of municipal waste

Country	Waste per person per year (kg)	(lbs)
1 USA	720	(1,587)
2 Australia	690	(1,521)
3 Iceland	650	(1,433)
4 New Zealand	635	(1,400)
5 Switzerland	600	(1,323)
6 Norway	600	(1,323)
7 Luxembourg	590	(1,301)
8 France	590	(1,301)
9 Netherlands	560	(1,234)
10 Denmark	560	(1,234)

Germany is 12th, Canada 14th, and the UK 18th

Source: OECD

What a load of rubbish!

- In the USA, the total amount of waste generated every day is more than twice the total weight of the entire population of 280 million.
- In the UK, on average, each person throws away seven times their own bodyweight in waste per year.
- In the USA, some 2.5 million plastic containers are thrown away every hour.
- In the UK, over 70 million metal food or drink cans are thrown away every day.
- In the USA, over 7 million cars and 250 million tyres are scrapped every year.
- In the UK in one year, enough household waste is generated to fill dustbins stretching all the way from the Earth to the Moon and back.

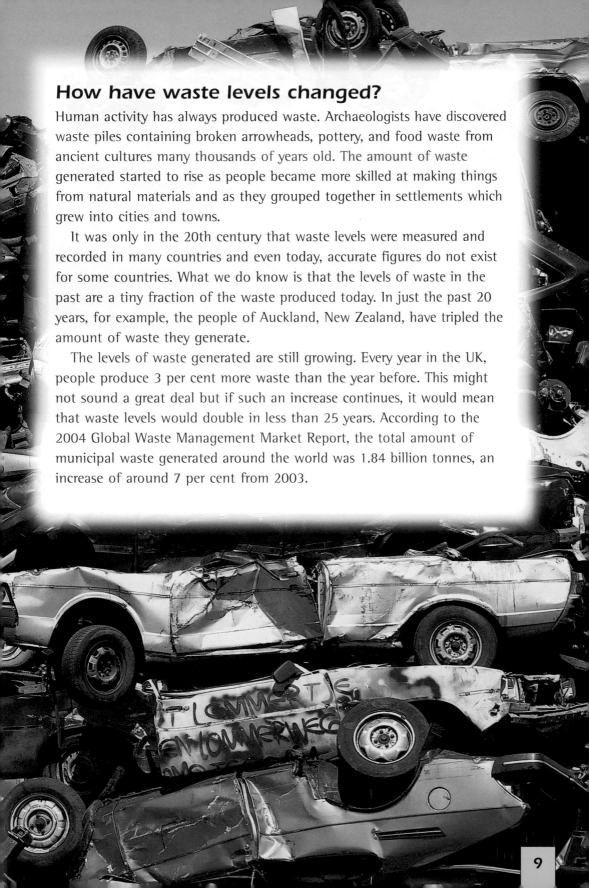

How have waste levels changed?

Human activity has always produced waste. Archaeologists have discovered waste piles containing broken arrowheads, pottery, and food waste from ancient cultures many thousands of years old. The amount of waste generated started to rise as people became more skilled at making things from natural materials and as they grouped together in settlements which grew into cities and towns.

It was only in the 20th century that waste levels were measured and recorded in many countries and even today, accurate figures do not exist for some countries. What we do know is that the levels of waste in the past are a tiny fraction of the waste produced today. In just the past 20 years, for example, the people of Auckland, New Zealand, have tripled the amount of waste they generate.

The levels of waste generated are still growing. Every year in the UK, people produce 3 per cent more waste than the year before. This might not sound a great deal but if such an increase continues, it would mean that waste levels would double in less than 25 years. According to the 2004 Global Waste Management Market Report, the total amount of municipal waste generated around the world was 1.84 billion tonnes, an increase of around 7 per cent from 2003.

Increasing populations, increasing waste

A booming human population is one major cause of the increase in waste. There are now 6.4 billion people living on the planet – more than eight times the total 250 years ago. People generate waste from their own bodies as well as from their activities to produce food, shelter, energy sources, transport, and thousands of other goods and services. For example, today the US generates the most waste. Its population has grown dramatically from 82 million in 1904 to 293 million in 2004.

However, this is only part of the picture. Not only are there many more people on the planet but, on average, each person is generating far more waste than in the past. Industries, particularly in more developed nations, mass produce vast numbers of products which people buy, use, and discard. Many products are designed to be disposable. It is often cheaper to buy a new replacement than to repair an old product. In addition, many products come with large amounts of packaging which is usually just thrown away.

Growth of waste in the USA

Year	Total waste per year	Per person per day (kg)	(lb)
1960	79.9 million tonnes	1.22	2.69
1970	109.9 million tonnes	1.49	3.28
1980	137.5 million tonnes	1.68	3.7
1990	186.2 million tonnes	2.04	4.5
2001	207.9 million tonnes	2.01	4.43

Source: *United States Environmental Protection Agency (EPA)*

Litter in Britain

The "Tidy Britain" campaign estimates that Britons drop over 23 million tonnes of litter every year. Almost all of this is food and drink packaging. Just 40 years ago, the figure was estimated to be around 5 million tonnes. In the UK, some 8 billion plastic carrier bags are given away every year, whilst hundreds of millions of plastic crisp bags are left to litter the streets. Each plastic bag takes many years to rot away.

The "Tidy Britain" logo is a simple symbol used to remind people to dispose of their rubbish in the correct manner.

Do levels of waste vary around the world?

Levels of waste vary greatly around the world. At one extreme is the USA, which produces around 20 per cent of the entire world's waste, yet contains less than 6 per cent of the world's population. The average person in the USA generates around 2 kilograms (4.4 pounds) of solid waste a day, whilst the average person in the Philippines generates just 400 grams (14 ounces). In many poor nations in Africa and Asia, the amount of waste generated is as low as 100–200 grams (3.5–7 ounces). Much of this difference comes down to wealth. People who live in wealthier, more developed nations tend to consume more goods and services which, in turn, tend to create more and more waste. In wealthier countries such as Australia, the US, Canada, and the nations of Western Europe, the average income is over US$20,000 per year. In Ethiopia, the average income is just US$108.

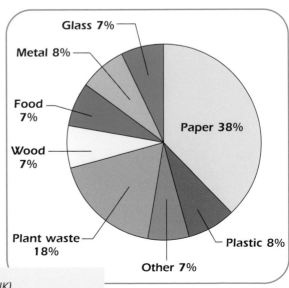

Typical contents of household solid waste (UK)
[Source: *Waste Disposal* (Sally Morgan, Franklin Watts)]

The waste problem today

A sustainable way of life is one in which **resources**, goods, and services are produced and used in ways which can be continued by people in the future. Sustainability in waste means generating as little waste as possible by reducing the amount of resources used, reusing materials, and by **recycling**. Generating vast amounts of waste is not a sustainable way of living because this waste can cause major health risks, generate **pollution**, and damage the environment. In addition, when something is not reused or recycled we lose the natural resources, the energy, and the time which have been used to make the product or material.

The Earth's resources are often divided into those which can reoccur (**renewable**), like the energy from the Sun, and those which are of a fixed quantity (non-renewable), such as the metals contained in rocks in the Earth. Some non-renewable resources such as **fossil fuels** (coal, **natural gas**, and oil) are being used up fast. Reserves of oil may only last another 40 to 50 years.

Other renewable resources like water, trees, or fish are under threat from their rapid and wasteful use by humans. Water can be polluted by waste, making it unfit to drink or unable to support life. Over-fishing in some areas has resulted in fish stocks reaching all-time lows. In just the last 40 years, over 40 per cent of the world's trees have been cut down to clear land or to provide timber or firewood. Given time, renewable resources can grow again, but not at the speed they are currently being used.

The world demand for paper runs into millions of tonnes every year. Much of the paper we use is made from wood. It takes around 75,000 trees to provide enough paper to print the 1.67 million copies of a Sunday edition of the New York Times *newspaper. Many of these newspapers are not recycled, so they end up as litter or as waste in dustbins.*

The costs of dealing with waste

Waste collection and disposal uses up yet more valuable resources, such as energy and land. In France, an estimated 15 per cent of all freight transport on land is the moving around of different types of waste. Giant rubbish dumps and landfill sites occupy large areas of land which potentially could be used for other purposes. The collection and disposal of waste is a major industry. It costs governments huge sums of money. In the USA, it costs an average of US$80 to dispose of one tonne of solid waste by burying or burning it. This may not sound much, but when it is multiplied by the 230 million tonnes of solid waste produced every year in the USA, it becomes a huge sum. In Japan, about 5 per cent of the total local government budget is spent on collecting and disposing of municipal waste. In poorer countries, it can cost 30 per cent or more of a local council's budget. These costs mean that less money can go to other vital services.

Pollution and health risks

Waste and the ways it is disposed of can generate pollution on land, in water, and in the air. Solid waste, burned in giant **incinerators**, can release harmful gases and particles into the **atmosphere**. Air pollution, especially in large towns and cities, is responsible for many illnesses.

Solid waste placed in poorly maintained landfill sites or just dumped outside can cause massive problems. In Bangladesh, for example, millions of plastic bags blocked drains, helping to prolong the 1998 floods which submerged almost two-thirds of the country. Solid waste clogging drains can also create non-moving, stagnant water – ideal breeding conditions for insects which carry diseases such as malaria. Plastic items, such as wire, carrier bags, and the plastic rings which hold together packs of cans, can trap or strangle mammals, birds, and sea creatures. An estimated 1 million sea birds die every year through eating, or being trapped by, plastic products.

Bangladesh is a low-lying country prone to severe flooding. Waste is adding to the problems there, preventing floodwaters from draining away.

Between 1953 and 1967, a fertilizer factory regularly deposited waste containing mercury in Minamata Bay, Japan. Over 20,000 people were poisoned and suffered blindness and brain damage. An estimated 40–50 people died.

Water and waste

Seas, rivers, and lakes have often been used as dumping grounds for waste from industry and from sewage systems. Tens of thousands of fish were killed in the Tisza River in Eastern Europe in 2000 when a gold mine leaked waste containing the poison cyanide into the river. Other creatures which feed on contaminated plants or animals can also be harmed or die. Waste in water can also make it unfit to drink, wash food with, or bathe in, and can carry harmful diseases such as **cholera**.

Waste and whales

Despite the 1979 ban on hunting, the number of endangered Beluga whales found in Canada's St Lawrence River estuary, has barely risen in 25 years. For over half a century, the estuary has been a dumping ground for industrial wastes, fertilizers, and **pesticides**. Rivers have carried more waste from the US and Canadian industries of the Great Lakes region. Studies have shown that whales can contain high levels of toxic substances including lead, mercury, and pesticides. Scientists believe that these pollutants have caused disease and reduced the ability of the whales to breed. The whales have been contaminated to such a high level that some Beluga whale carcasses are considered hazardous waste themselves.

What types of waste are there?

Waste can be grouped in a number of different ways. It can be divided into materials which can or cannot rot into the earth, or by whether the waste is a solid, liquid, or gas. Another way of dividing up waste is based on its source. Common types of waste include agricultural waste, industrial waste, municipal solid waste, and sewage.

Municipal solid waste (MSW) is generated by a town or region's houses, schools, offices, and hospitals. It includes large, discarded goods such as furniture, fridges, and computers. It also includes grass cuttings and garden waste, food waste, discarded metal, plastic, and clothing. In the UK alone, some 7.5 billion items of clothing are thrown away every year.

The make-up of municipal solid waste varies greatly between countries. In the most developed nations, paper and card, particularly from newspapers, mail, and packaging, form the largest part of MSW. In poorer, less developed nations most waste is food and plant waste, such as corn husks or other parts of plants which cannot be eaten.

Abandonded fridges are difficult to dispose of. Often they lie rusting in tips for years.

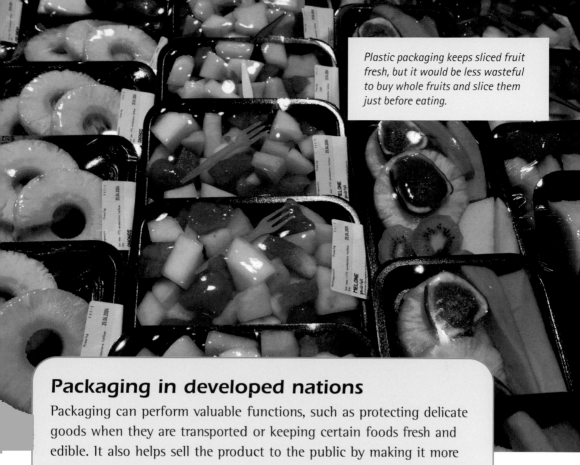

Plastic packaging keeps sliced fruit fresh, but it would be less wasteful to buy whole fruits and slice them just before eating.

Packaging in developed nations

Packaging can perform valuable functions, such as protecting delicate goods when they are transported or keeping certain foods fresh and edible. It also helps sell the product to the public by making it more convenient to use or more attractive to look at. However, many people think that a lot of packaging, such as over individual fruits and vegetables, is unnecessary and wasteful. In the UK, an estimated 9.3 million tonnes of waste packaging is generated per year; that's 25,000 tonnes every day, or 157 kg (346 lb) of packaging for every person living in the UK. In the USA, 28.8 million tonnes of waste corrugated cardboard boxes alone are created every year.

Composition of municipal solid waste in USA and Uganda

	USA (% of total)	Uganda (% of total)
Paper	4	5.4
Plant and food	25	81.8
Metal	9	3.1
Plastic	8	1.6
Glass	7	0.9
Others	11	7.2

[Source: *Waste Recycling and Reuse* (Rob Bowden, Hodder Wayland)]

What is E-waste?

E-waste is a type of municipal solid waste (MSW) which is rapidly growing in more developed nations. E-waste consists of audio, video, computing, and telecommunications goods which are thrown away when considered **obsolete**, even if they are still working. In the USA, E-waste is an increasing problem with over 2 million tonnes generated every year. These items are made up of a large range of different materials which makes recycling difficult. They also include potentially harmful materials such as lead and **cadmium.**

Composition of E-Waste in the United States, 2000

Equipment	Weight (tonnes)	Percentage of total
TVs	1,181,166	55.60
Packaging	380,267	17.90
Commercial electronics	214,564	10.10
Household electronics	129,588	6.10
Monitors	125,339	5.90
PCs	93,473	4.40

Where does industrial waste come from?

Industrial waste comes from a range of sources. The waste materials created when goods, such as cars, computers, or processed foods are manufactured is one source. Another significant source is industrial wastewater. Water is used by factories to cool factory machinery and the products they make, to dilute chemicals, and to clean items. After use, the wastewater is often pumped back into rivers or the sea, even though it may still contain waste substances.

As many as 15 million mobile phones are discarded in the UK every year as users trade-up to newer models. The old phones can degrade and leak potentially dangerous waste substances such as lead.

Amongst the biggest waste-generating industries is mining, which produces vast amounts of unwanted material dug out of the ground, called tailings. When mining for precious metals such as gold or platinum, as much as 99 per cent of all mined rock and soil is waste. Some of this waste material is washed away from the valuable metal at a mine or a metal mill and may find its way back into rivers and lakes. There, it can settle and build up as **sediment**, especially on the beds of slow rivers and harbour waters. Dredging is the removal of this sediment in order to allow shipping to safely travel through. The material removed is known as dredged spoils and can contain toxic substances.

RADIOACTIVE

RADIOACTIVE

RADIOAC

These containers of industrial radioactive waste are beginning to rust; the contents could cause great damage to the environment if they were to leak out.

Sewage and wastewater

On average, in the West, each person generates 150–200 grams (5–7 ounces) of solid waste and 1.2 litres (0.3 gallons) of liquid waste every day. Water is used to flush away and carry most human wastes, as well as household waste from showers, baths, washing machines, and toilets. This wastewater will eventually reach rivers, lakes, or seas. In wealthier, more developed countries, it is first cleaned at a sewage treatment plant (see diagram below). But this is an expensive process. In many countries, it is too expensive to build and run treatment plants and almost all sewage runs untreated into rivers, lakes, and seas. There it can pollute the water and cause disease.

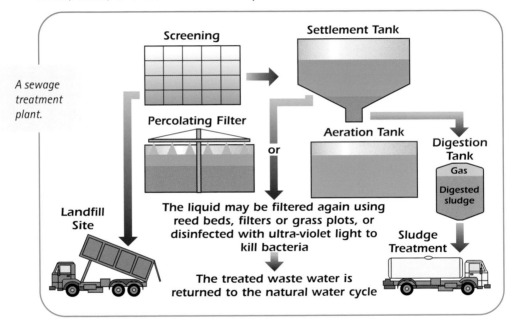

A sewage treatment plant.

Screening

Settlement Tank

Percolating Filter

or

Aeration Tank

Digestion Tank

Gas

Digested sludge

Landfill Site

The liquid may be filtered again using reed beds, filters or grass plots, or disinfected with ultra-violet light to kill bacteria

Sludge Treatment

The treated waste water is returned to the natural water cycle

Number of people with no access to improved sanitation

Country	Percentage of population	Approximate number
Rwanda	88	6.4 million
Afghanistan	75	20.1 million
Cambodia	44	5.5 million
India	39	397 million
China	31	394 million
Rumania	15	3.3 million
UK and USA	less than 0.1	–

[Source: *United Nations Millennium Indicators* (UN Population Statistics)]

What makes up hazardous waste?

Hazardous wastes are materials and items which are a threat to the environment or human health. **Industrialized** countries produce nearly 80 per cent of the 400 million tonnes of hazardous waste estimated to be generated every year. Most hazardous wastes come from industry, but household hazardous waste (HHW) exists and includes old medicines, paints, car anti-freeze, **disinfectants**, and other cleaning products. **Radioactive** wastes from industry, medicine, and scientific research are amongst the most hazardous of all wastes and have to be specially disposed of. Agriculture also generates significant amounts of hazardous waste in the form of harmful chemicals designed to kill insects (pesticides) and weeds (herbicides).

Waste pesticide stockpiles

An estimated 60,000 tonnes of out-of-date pesticides have built up in stockpiles throughout Africa and the Middle East. Some of these stockpiles are unmanaged, or details of where they are located have been lost. Many have littered areas near villages and farmlands with rusting and leaking barrels of dangerous waste. This waste has entered the soil and water used by rural villages, poisoning these vital resources. Hundreds of families in Ethiopia, Mali, and other African nations have been forced to abandon their homes and move to new areas.

Waste pesticide stockpiles

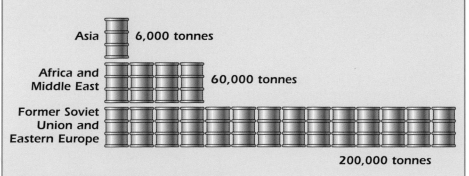

Asia — 6,000 tonnes

Africa and Middle East — 60,000 tonnes

Former Soviet Union and Eastern Europe — 200,000 tonnes

Source: United Nations FAO

What happens to waste?

"Waste management" means collecting and disposing of waste. In wealthy, more developed nations, many millions of dollars are spent on waste management. People there tend to take for granted that waste is collected and disposed of. In many less wealthy countries, solid waste is often simply dumped on the surface and left to rot. In some cities in Africa, Asia, and South America, between 20 per cent and 50 per cent of solid waste is left on the streets. This rotting waste can spread disease.

In the Philippines life goes on amongst the piles of rubbish.

Living in a dump

Payatas is the largest waste dump in the Philippines and is situated on the outskirts of Quezon City. Every day, 500 trucks deposit over 3,000 tonnes of rubbish at the site. Some 60,000 people, many of them children, live off this rubbish, scavenging for plastic, metal, glass, and any other materials or items which can be sold to recycling businesses. It is unpleasant, tiring, and dangerous work. The air is filled with the fumes of rotting materials, whilst broken glass and rusting metal can cut hands and feet. There is also the risk of catching a disease such as dysentery, **tetanus**, or **cholera**, or coming into contact with dangerous toxic waste mixed in with the regular rubbish. In July 2000, a massive landslide on part of the giant dump buried a 300-home makeshift village on the site, killing at least 280 people. Yet, many of those who live and work there feel they have little alternative.

Methods of waste disposal

Most of the waste collected from schools, houses, and offices in wealthier countries is managed in one of four ways:

- buried in landfill sites
- composted
- burned
- recycled in some way.

For many years, burying waste in landfill sites has been the most common treatment for solid waste. In the USA, just over half of all municipal solid waste is buried in landfill sites. It is estimated that a quarter of all landfill space in the USA is taken up by waste packaging. In the UK, around 75 per cent of solid waste is buried, a further 9 per cent is **incinerated**, and 16 per cent composted or recycled.

Percentage of waste in the USA disposed of by different means

Waste disposal method	1960	1970	1980	1990	2000	2005
Recycled/composted	6.4	6.6	9.6	16.2	30	32
Incinerated	30.6	20.7	9.0	15.5	16.7	15.9
Landfilled	63	72.6	81.4	68.3	53.3	52.1

Source: *US Environmental Protection Agency (EPA)*

Illegal dumping

Figures from governments and official sources do not always give the whole picture. Many tonnes of waste of different types are often illegally dumped. Sometimes this is done by companies wanting to avoid the high costs of disposing of **toxic wastes** at proper sites. The exact levels of illegal dumping are hard to measure, but the costs of cleaning this waste up are recorded. In the city of Los Angeles, for example, local government spends over US$4 million every year cleaning up approximately 121,000 tons of illegally dumped solid waste.

What is composting?

As much as a third of the waste in a household dustbin consists of material which was once living and which can **biodegrade** relatively quickly. This material includes grass cuttings, tea bags, and other non-cooked food waste. This material can be put in a **compost** bin where it rots down to form compost, which is an excellent natural **fertilizer**.

Household compost bins can provide families with useful supplies of compost whilst cutting down their household waste. On a larger scale, commercial composting sites can turn large quantities of biodegradable waste, which would otherwise be burned or buried, into useful materials (such as potting/garden compost). The sites use relatively little energy and labour. In Chelson Meadow landfill in the UK city of Plymouth, for instance, every 100 tonnes of municipal solid waste received is turned into around 49 tonnes of compost suitable for farmers and landscapers.

Old TVs, fridges, cars, and waste rubble from building work are all commonly abandoned by roadsides, where they form unsightly and polluting piles.

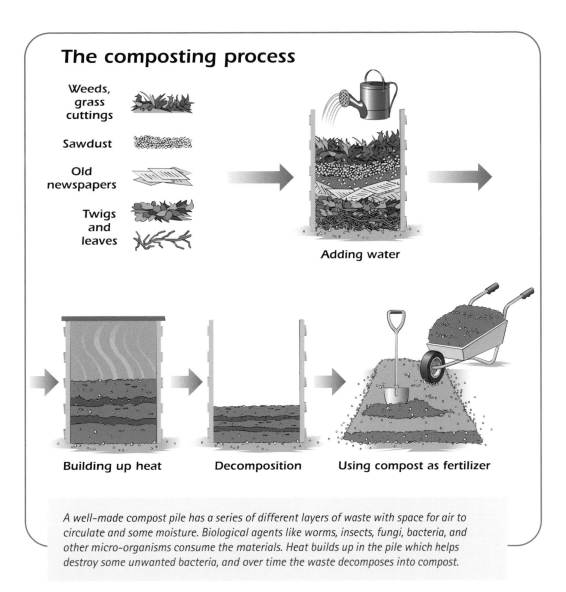

The composting process

Weeds, grass cuttings

Sawdust

Old newspapers

Twigs and leaves

Adding water

Building up heat

Decomposition

Using compost as fertilizer

A well-made compost pile has a series of different layers of waste with space for air to circulate and some moisture. Biological agents like worms, insects, fungi, bacteria, and other micro-organisms consume the materials. Heat builds up in the pile which helps destroy some unwanted bacteria, and over time the waste decomposes into compost.

What are landfill sites?

Landfill sites are essentially giant holes in the ground in which solid municipal waste and waste from mining, construction, and other industries can be dumped. In the past, landfill sites were large, unlined holes filled with rubbish squashed down by machinery which, when full, were covered in soil and turned into parks, common land, or golf courses. Today, modern sanitary landfill sites are carefully engineered constructions, divided into cells, each with a liner to prevent waste materials seeping into the soil and underground water supplies. In Australia today, 14 million tonnes of waste are buried in landfills, three quarters of a tonne for every Australian.

GIVING OFF GASES

As many forms of organic waste rot in a landfill they produce gases, particularly carbon dioxide and methane. Methane burns easily and is highly explosive and there is a threat of fire and explosion at some landfill sites. Underground fires at landfill sites can burn for long periods, sending pollutants into the air. Some 9 million waste motor vehicle tyres are buried in a landfill at Heyope in Powys, Wales. An underground fire that started there in 1989 was still burning in 2002! The methane from a large landfill can generate enough electricity to power 6,000 or more homes. But most of the remainder enters the **atmosphere**, where it plays a part in the **enhanced greenhouse effect** believed to be behind **global warming**.

WHAT IS LEACHATE?

Rainwater or floodwater can seep through waste at a landfill site helping to dissolve and carry substances from the waste. These substances can come from **pesticides**, acids from leaking batteries and, occasionally, chemicals from oils, paint solvents, and cleaning compounds. This mixture of substances can be harmful and is known as **leachate**. At an unmaintained or old landfill, leachate can seep into the surrounding soil, underground water supplies, or nearby rivers and streams. Modern landfill sites have leachate collection pipes which carry most of the leachate away for treatment, but they are expensive and need constant maintenance.

Excess gas produced at landfill sites is often burned off and not put to practical use.

The world's biggest landfill site

On Staten Island close to New York City lies the world's largest landfill facility. Called Fresh Kills, it was open from 1948 to 2001 and at its peak received around 4.3 million tonnes of solid waste every year. The waste is spread over a number of mounds covering much of the 1,214-hectare site and standing taller than the Statue of Liberty. The dump gives off a number of gases including an estimated 5 per cent of the entire US emissions of methane. In addition, millions of litres of toxic leachate flow into New York harbour every year. Although the site is now slowly being landscaped and some methane and leachate collected, the environmental effects remain.

WHAT OTHER PROBLEMS EXIST WITH LANDFILLS?

Landfills occupy a great deal of space and many current landfill sites are nearly full. Densely populated countries are running out of suitable space for new landfills whilst public resistance to landfills is rising. Many forms of solid waste do not biodegrade well in a landfill whilst poorly managed sites can lead to dust, odour, flies, and other pests making life unpleasant for nearby residents. To some people, though, the key problem with landfills is that they are full of wasted resources which are buried and lost, rather than recovered, reused, or recycled.

Burning waste

Burning solid waste in specially designed incinerators has both advantages and drawbacks. The heat generated kills micro-organisms which carry disease, whilst filters and other devices reduce the amount of polluting gases and particles released into the air. **Incineration** reduces the weight of the solid waste by 75 per cent and the amount of space it takes up by as much as 90 per cent. In energy from waste (EfW) incinerators, the heat released from the burning of solid waste can be used to heat nearby buildings or turn water into steam to power electricity generators. In 2001, the USA had 97 EfW incinerators but incineration is unpopular with the American people. Between 1985 and 1998, plans for over 300 new incinerator projects were put on hold or defeated due to a lack of public support.

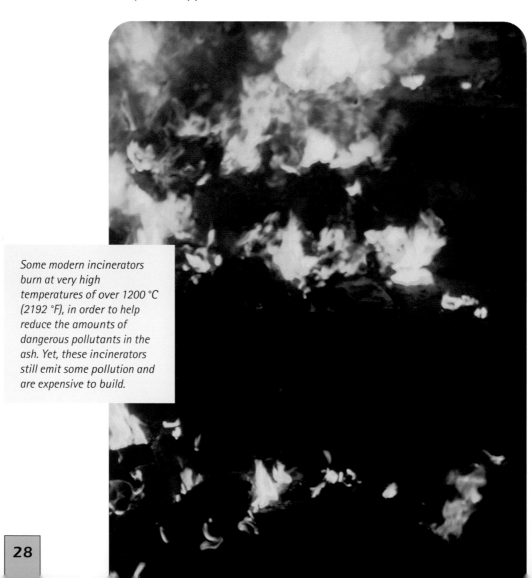

Some modern incinerators burn at very high temperatures of over 1200 °C (2192 °F), in order to help reduce the amounts of dangerous pollutants in the ash. Yet, these incinerators still emit some pollution and are expensive to build.

Percentage of municipal waste incinerated in selected countries	
Australia	less than 2%
UK	9%
USA	16%
France	20%
The Netherlands	20%
Norway	32.5%

The technology to burn waste has improved in the past 40 years but all incinerators emit polluting gases, such as sulphur dioxide and nitrous oxide, into the atmosphere. Substantial amounts of ash remain after burning which can contain residues of toxic chemicals. Other pollutants generated by incineration include small but noticeable amounts of poisonous lead, **cadmium**, mercury, and **particulates**.

Most health concerns about incineration have focused on a family of chemicals called "**dioxins**". There are over 200 different dioxins and, according to the United Nations Environmental Programme, 17 of them are highly toxic. Dioxins can build up in the fatty tissues of people and other living things and studies have shown they can cause cancer, disrupt humans' nervous systems, and weaken their immune systems. Municipal waste incinerators were the biggest source of dioxins in the USA in the late 1990s.

What happens to hazardous waste?

Hazardous waste produced in industry, research, and medicine poses extra problems in its disposal. Much medical waste is burned in specialized incinerators, whilst other waste is treated with chemicals to reduce its threat before being burned in regular incinerators or buried in regular landfill sites. Some hazardous waste is buried in specialist hazardous waste sites. In 2001, a study by Imperial College, London, found that birth defects were a little more likely in babies born near these sites. Extremely high levels of dioxins and other harmful wastes from chemicals industries were found in the Russian city of Dzerzhinsk; these contributed to the city's average life expectancy being nearly seventeen years shorter than the national average.

EXPORTING WASTE

To comply with their own stricter environmental laws and increasing public concern at home, many wealthier nations are transporting hazardous waste to other countries for disposal. Canada, for example, receives over 85 per cent of the hazardous waste that the USA sends out. Environmentalists are worried that in other cases, waste is sent to poorer countries who need the money paid as a treatment fee, but who will not, or cannot, dispose of it safely.

Faced with the costs and problems of disposing of hazardous waste, some companies choose to dump the waste secretly and illegally at sea or on land. One Japanese company dumped hazardous waste on the small Japanese island of Teshima for 17 years until stopped by police in 1991. The cleanup operation is estimated to have cost over US$300 million.

Leper ships

Ships moving hazardous waste from country to country have been dubbed "leper ships" by the world's media and often travel for many months seeking a home for their cargo. One of the most notorious leper ships, the *Khian Sea*, set sail from Philadelphia, USA, in 1986 carrying over 14,000 tonnes of regular incinerator ash. Country after country refused to accept the ash and in 1988, some of the waste was dumped on a beach in Haiti. The ship underwent two changes of name and sailed on to Africa and Asia but after refusals from 15 nations, the ash

was dumped at sea. This was not the end of the story. Most of the ash dumped in Haiti was finally transported back to the USA and sat on a barge off the coast of Florida for many months. It was finally buried in a new landfill site back in Philadelphia in 2002.

In 1999, the leper ship MV Ulla *carried waste ash from power stations in Spain but its original destination, Algeria, refused its cargo, as did Turkey. Moored off the Turkish coast for four years, the ship mysteriously sank in September 2004, taking its 2,400-tonne cargo with it.*

RADIOACTIVE WASTE

Radioactive waste poses special problems as the radiation it emits can cause harm to living things for long periods of time. Waste is graded according to how radioactive it is. Low-level waste's radioactivity may fade in 40 or 50 years and is often placed inside metal drums and buried. Intermediate and high-level waste's radioactivity is much more powerful and may last thousands of years.

Much controversy surrounds how this waste should be finally disposed of. Many countries have plans to build deep underground stores for high-level waste, but the engineering problems of trying to protect this waste from natural disasters for as long as 100,000 years are immense.

Scientists use sensors to test for possible radiation emissions from stored containers of radioactive waste.

Solving waste problems

Many people believe that much of our waste is either unnecessary or could be reduced. The waste hierarchy (below) shows the many ways waste can be dealt with. For example, millions of motor vehicle tyres are worn out every year. Many are dumped in landfill sites as waste, millions more are burned to recover energy to power factories. Tyres can be re-treaded so that they can be reused, or turned into a sort of rubber crumb which can be used for sports and playground surfaces and carpet underlay. Other tyres are reused as playground swings or as "bumpers" for harbour walls and boats.

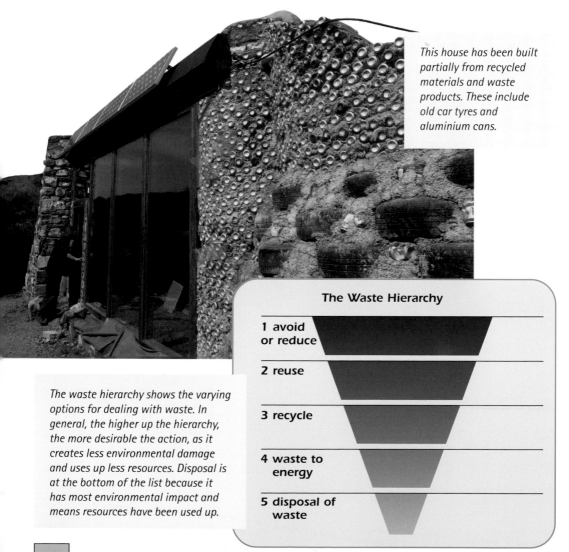

This house has been built partially from recycled materials and waste products. These include old car tyres and aluminium cans.

The waste hierarchy shows the varying options for dealing with waste. In general, the higher up the hierarchy, the more desirable the action, as it creates less environmental damage and uses up less resources. Disposal is at the bottom of the list because it has most environmental impact and means resources have been used up.

The Waste Hierarchy

1 avoid or reduce

2 reuse

3 recycle

4 waste to energy

5 disposal of waste

What happens to waste tyres in selected countries? (percentage)

	USA	Japan	Germany	UK	Australia
Landfill/stockpile	74	11	30	53	66
Energy recovery	7	35	37	20	0
Re-treaded	12	12	19	19	27
Export	2	22	2	0	2
Crumbed	4	22	2	0	0
Other uses	1	3	1	2	5

[Source: Australian Department of the Environment and Heritage]

How can fewer materials be used?

Avoiding or reducing waste would solve the problems and costs of waste disposal and preserve resources for future generations. This is known as "waste minimization".

Industry has taken many steps in waste minimization in the past 30 years. Computer-based design and technology has enabled goods to be made using fewer materials. A modern car, for example, weighs many kilograms less than one from the 1960s, in part due to using less steel in its **chassis** and panels. The idea of making products using fewer materials is called "light-weighting" and has been applied to many types of plastic, glass, and metal containers. For example, aluminium cans are 30 per cent lighter than they were 25 years ago. Using fewer materials helps not only to cut down the amounts used in production but also saves energy in transportation. Many feel, though, that industry could do more, such as to make goods which are easier to repair and last longer.

For consumers, waste minimization can mean making careful buying choices, buying less, buying items that last longer, and replacing items only when necessary.

Some people point to the fact that waste created by households is only a fraction of the total amount. However, the products which make up household waste have already used up many additional resources and generated much more waste along the way. Waste has been generated in the manufacture of a product, in its packaging, and as it is transported to consumers.

How are products and materials reused?

Reusing a product extends its life and prevents it from heading into the bin as waste. The product can be reused for the exact same purpose as before – i.e. returning milk bottles or printer ink cartridges for refilling, or selling an old but working computer to another user. Products can be reused for a slightly different purpose, such as an empty jam jar for storing other food, or a product can be used in a totally different way. In a number of African nations, old, empty oil drums have been cut in half and had old pram or bicycle wheels attached to make a trailer to transport food, water, and even passengers around.

Today, thanks to charities such as Computer Aid, 50 per cent of students leave Swaziland schools computer-literate.

Reuse of computers

In 1998, 99 per cent of students in the African nation of Swaziland left school never having seen a computer. In wealthier nations, people and companies may change their PCs every two years, generating an enormous amount of E-waste. Computer Aid is one of a number of charities which takes old, unwanted computers from big business and ships them to schools and community projects in poorer nations, particularly in Africa. The charity has already shipped over 45,000 machines and plans to reuse 50,000 PCs a year from its headquarters.

What is recycling?

Recycling is an important form of waste recovery. Waste materials are collected and made into new products or materials. New aluminium cans can be made out of old ones. Plastic bottles can be cleaned and shredded and used as raw material to make bin liners and other new products. Composting is considered a form of natural recycling, creating valuable soil-enhancing material out of old food and garden waste.

Percentage of waste recycled in selected countries

Austria	50
Germany	46
The Netherlands	43
Canada	42
Denmark	29
Sweden	28.5
USA	28
UK	11
Ireland	9
France	7
Italy	3
Spain	3

[Source: Institute of Wastes Management]

Materials need to be collected, transported to centres where they are sorted, and then undergo recycling processes. These actions can use up energy and other resources, but often the cost is worth it. Firstly, recycling can dramatically reduce the amount of waste that has to be handled, transported, and disposed of. Secondly, recycling can reduce the amounts of new resources used up. Thirdly, recycling often takes far less energy to produce a useful material than making the material from scratch. This reduction in energy use means less pollution in the air and water.

Recycling one tonne of glass can save up to 135 litres (35 gallons) of oil used as a fuel to make glass from scratch.

To produce a tonne of aluminium requires 5 tonnes of a rocky ore called bauxite and over 16,000 kilowatt-hours of electricity. But to recycle a tonne of old aluminium cans, in contrast, needs only 750 kilowatt-hours. Creating one tonne of recycled paper uses 64 per cent less energy, 50 per cent less water, generates over 70 per cent less air pollution, and saves 17 trees, compared with producing the same amount of paper from new trees.

Energy savings by recycling materials

Material	Energy saved compared to producing new material
Recycled aluminium	95%
Recycled copper	85%
Recycled plastics	80%
Recycled steel	74%
Recycled lead	65%
Recycled paper	64%

Why isn't more waste recycled?

Although recycling has many benefits, the vast majority of countries recycle well under half of their waste. Sometimes, this is due to technical issues of separating and sorting materials. Plastics recycling, for example, can be difficult. There are dozens of different plastics and often a product will contain many plastics as well as other materials, making it hard to recycle. Dismantling complex products like electronic goods can be too time-consuming and expensive for it to be considered worthwhile. Some materials, particularly lightweight plastic food wrappers and plastic PET bottles used for soft drinks, are extremely light and bulky. This makes them hard to collect in sufficient quantity for recycling. It takes 20,000 PET bottles, for example, to make one tonne of recycled plastic.

Sometimes, there are concerns about the quality of recycled materials. For example, paper degrades in quality each time it is recycled and can only be recycled four or so times. After that the fibres are too short and weak to be used again. On other occasions, the problem is one of governments not promoting or enforcing recycling. Many governments have not invested the money to build enough recycling containers and centres.

Changing the attitudes of consumers is also vital if more waste is to be recycled. Millions of people either don't care or cannot be bothered to sort their rubbish or take recyclable products to local centres. They also choose not to use products which cut back on waste or are recycled. Modern rechargeable batteries, for example, can be reused at least 1,000 times, but their higher cost and the inconvenience of recharging batteries mean that regular batteries are still used heavily. Americans, for example, throw away 2.5 billion batteries a year.

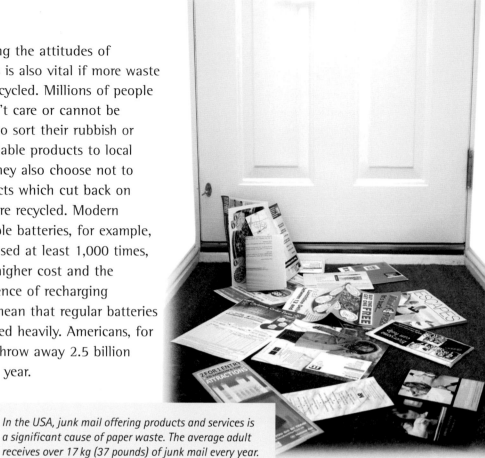

In the USA, junk mail offering products and services is a significant cause of paper waste. The average adult receives over 17 kg (37 pounds) of junk mail every year. If just one million of these people stopped their junk mail, it would save about 1.5 million trees a year.

Best and worst in western Europe

The UK lags behind most of western Europe in its waste recycling. The UK's recycling rate has increased from 2.9 per cent in 1990 to 11 per cent in the 21st century, but is almost 40 per cent behind Austria. The UK has failed to reach two 2005 European Union targets – recycling 50 per cent of all packaging, and reducing waste going to landfill by 25 per cent. Austria, in contrast, has one of the highest recycling rates in the world. It recycles more than 45 per cent of its plastic, 75 per cent of its steel cans, and collects 84 per cent of all its glass containers for reuse or recycling. It has over 880,000 recycling containers, many more than the UK, despite having a fifth of the population of the UK. In 2004, it also passed a new law allowing no plastic in landfill sites.

Taxes and fines on waste

A number of national and local governments in the UK have recently imposed new taxes or costs on waste to help motivate people to recycle or consume less. In the Republic of Ireland, a tax on plastic bags, the PlasTax, was introduced in 2001. Within a year, official statistics showed that consumption of bags was down by 90 per cent. In the UK, a tax on every tonne of waste buried in landfill sites is in place. This tax rises each year. It is designed to encourage councils and businesses to find other ways of handling waste. But some critics claim that this tax is not high enough to encourage new recycling schemes, and may lead to much more illegal dumping.

Pay As You Throw

In the USA, more than 6,000 cities or communities have started Pay As You Throw (PAYT) schemes where people pay for each bag of rubbish they set out for disposal instead of paying a flat rate for as many bags as they like. This is designed to encourage people to create less waste. In the city of Fort Worth, Texas, recycling rates have jumped from just 6 per cent to 20 per cent in a year. However, critics fear that such tax schemes on waste may lead to an increase in illegal dumping to avoid the charges.

Recycling in Brazil

Some people feel that instead of charging consumers for waste disposal, a better way is to give them an incentive to recycle. In the city of Curitiba in Brazil, 10,000 poorer families participate in a "Garbage that is not Garbage" programme that began in 1989. They receive food for every 4 kilograms (8.8 pounds) of recyclable waste they collect and deliver to mobile recycling units. Brazil has the highest aluminium can recycling rates in the world, reaching almost 90 per cent of the 9.5 billion cans thrown away in 2003. This is partly due to education and recycling schemes put in place by aluminium companies, but also due to paying as many as 100,000 garbage pickers for the cans they recover and deliver for recycling. A full-time can collector can earn up to five times the country's minimum wage.

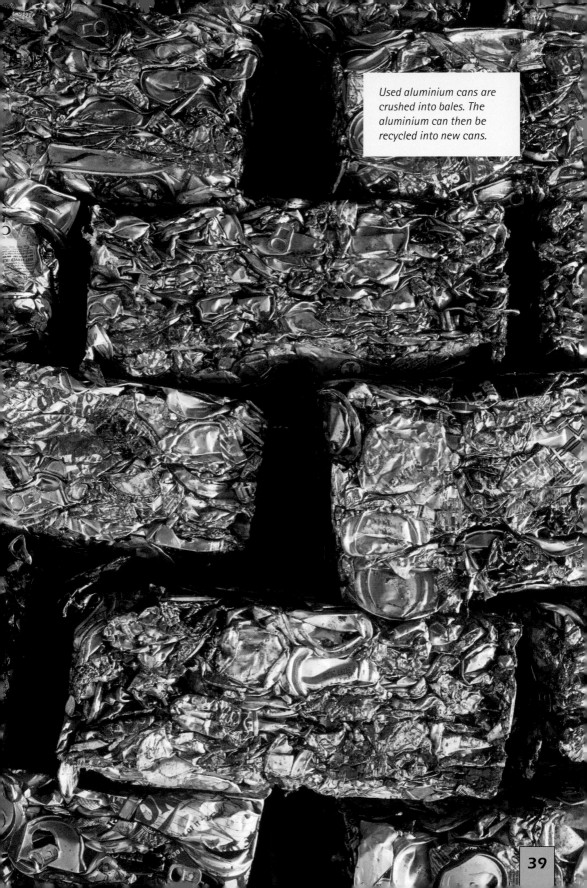

Used aluminium cans are crushed into bales. The aluminium can then be recycled into new cans.

The future

Waste is not going to go away. The world population is increasing by approximately 80 million every year, which means more consumption of more goods and even higher levels of waste. People in wealthy nations tend to consume more and generate far more waste than people in poorer nations. Many poorer countries in Africa, Asia, and South America are developing their industries, which means that more and more of their people will consume goods and generate waste. As waste levels rise, what remains of many of the planet's resources will decrease, whilst greater health and environmental problems will increase. Unless things change.

Some aspects of the waste issue are beginning to improve. For example, **composting** organic waste and **recycling** rates are increasing in many wealthy nations. The USA recycled 2.5 times more waste in 2004 than it did in 1990. It is expected to recycle a third of all its solid waste by 2006 but all countries need to recycle much more if the problem is to be tackled effectively.

Renewable energy which generates little **pollution** or waste may lead to a decrease in mining waste and waste oil products. Hydrogen **fuel cell** technology for motor vehicles may help reduce the world's current dependence on **fossil fuels**. Other technological breakthroughs in making products with less materials, or which can be recycled easily, may make an important contribution, as might new ways of reusing or converting old goods and materials into useful new ones.

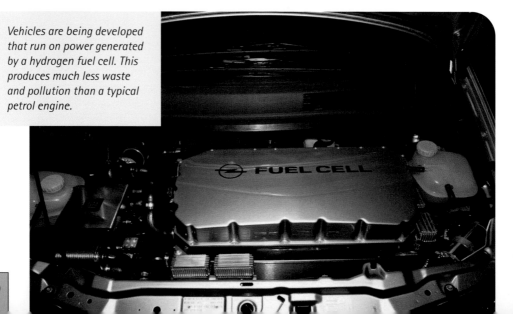

Vehicles are being developed that run on power generated by a hydrogen fuel cell. This produces much less waste and pollution than a typical petrol engine.

Perhaps what is most required is a change in the attitudes of individuals, industries, and governments to produce less waste in the first place, and ensure more materials and resources are reused and recycled. We can make a real difference by changing the way we buy and use products and by getting involved in home or local reusing and recycling schemes.

Buying loose fruit and vegetables in a market uses less packaging than buying prepared produce from a supermarket.

Ten things you can do to reduce waste

- Try to buy fruit and vegetables with as little packaging as possible.
- Take carrier bags with you when you go shopping rather than use new bags.
- Don't throw away clothes, toys, and other goods. Take them to thrift stores, charity shops, and special recycling programmes.
- If you want to buy an item, consider buying second-hand from adverts online or in newspapers, or from second-hand stores and charity shops.
- Reuse items whenever you can. For example, cut down old cereal boxes to use as document holders and reuse drinks bottles for packed lunches.
- Learn about your area's recycling schemes and recycle as much of your family's and school's waste as possible.
- Buy and use rechargeable batteries and fit energy efficient lightbulbs.
- Start a composting system in your garden or at school.
- Remove tops from plastic bottles and containers and crush them before depositing them at a recycling centre. This reduces the amount of space they take up which helps save on transport costs.
- Look at ways of using less water – by taking showers instead of baths and always turning off taps.

Statistical information

Uses of recovered paper in the USA

12,891,000 tons of printing and writing paper (42.1% of total) was recovered in the USA in 2001:

- 38.7%: exported abroad
- 21.7%: tissue
- 18.4%: recycled paperboard
- 11%: into new printing and writing paper
- 8.2%: other uses
- 2%: newsprint

[Source: Recovered Paper Statistical Highlights, 2002]

Aluminium can recycling in Europe and USA

Country	Percentage recycled
Switzerland	91
Sweden	85
Finland	84
Benelux*	80
Iceland	80
Norway	80
Germany	71
USA	63
Austria	50
UK	42
Spain	39
France	33

[Source: European Aluminium Association]

*Benelux = the countries of Belgium, the Netherlands, and Luxembourg.

Steel can and packaging recycling in selected countries 2003

Country	Percentage recycled
Belgium	94
Netherlands	82
Germany	80
Austria	79
Sweden	73
Switzerland	66
Norway	62
France	60
Spain	58
USA	57
UK	44.5
Australia	40

[Source: APEAL]

Top ten paper recycling countries

Country	Percentage recycled
Germany	72
South Korea	66
Sweden	55
Japan	53
Canada	47
USA	46
France	41
Finland	35
Italy	31
China	27

[Source: Vital Signs 2000]

Top consumers of recovered paper, 2001

Country	Tonnes
USA	30,163,887
China	17,361,698
Japan	14,914,114
Germany	10,456,209
South Korea	6,109,888
France	5,040,317
Italy	4,616,662
Canada	4,217,501
UK	4,183,935
Spain	3,807,453
Taiwan	3,375,633
Mexico	3,195,104
Brazil	2,384,988
Netherlands	2,362,308

[Source: Bureau International Recycling]

Waste produced per person in selected countries

Country	Waste produced per person per year (kg)	(lbs)
USA	720	(1,587)
Australia	690	(1,521)
Iceland	650	(1,433)
New Zealand	635	(1,400)
Switzerland	600	(1,322)
Luxembourg	590	(1,300)
France	590	(1,300)
The Netherlands	560	(1,234)
Denmark	560	(1,234)
Ireland	560	(1,234)
Germany	546	(1,203)
Austria	510	(1,124)
Canada	500	(1,102)
Belgium	480	(1,058)
UK	480	(1,058)
Italy	460	(1,014)
Portugal	440	(970)
Finland	410	(904)
Thailand	401	(884)
Singapore	401	(884)
Japan	400	(882)
South Korea	400	(882)
Saudi Arabia	400	(882)
Israel	400	(882)
Spain	390	(860)
Greece	370	(816)
Sweden	360	(794)
Turkey	330	(727)
Sri Lanka	321	(708)
Poland	320	(705)
Czech Republic	310	(683)
Mexico	310	(683)
Malaysia	295	(650)
China	288	(635)
Indonesia	277	(611)
Mongolia	219	(483)
Indonesia	215	(474)
Romania	215	(474)
Bulgaria	215	(474)
Vietnam	200	(441)
Colombia	198	(437)
The Philippines	189	(417)
Nepal	182	(401)
Bangladesh	179	(395)
India	168	(370)
Liberia	166	(366)
Kenya	166	(366)
Côte d'Ivoire	166	(366)
Trinidad & Tobago	166	(366)
Myanmar	164	(362)

[Sources: OECD, UNEP, World Bank]

43

Glossary

algae primitive plants, including green, brown, and red seaweeds and pond scums

atmosphere collection of gases that surround Earth

bacteria large group of different types of microscopic living things, some of which are useful to human activity, whilst others are harmful

biodegrade be broken down and recycled naturally in the environment

cadmium type of metal

chassis frame at the base of a car or truck

cholera infectious disease of the small intestine carried by bacteria

compost decayed living matter that can be used to fertilize the soil

consumer person who buys and uses goods and services

decompose become rotten and break down

dioxins group of extremely toxic chemicals produced during the making or disposal of certain products

disinfectant chemical or physical process that kills organisms, such as chlorine used to disinfect water

emission gas released into the air by industry, fires, and motor vehicles that is often harmful to health and the environment

endangered (species) species of living thing which is seriously threatened with extinction (dying out)

enhanced greenhouse effect build-up of gases in the atmosphere, trapping the sun's heat and affecting the climate

excrete discharge waste materials from the body

fertilizer substance which enriches soil and helps it support more plant life

fossil fuel material which can be burned to generate energy

fuel cell device which converts chemical energy into electrical energy and usually uses hydrogen as a fuel

global warming warming-up of Earth's surface due to changes in the gases which form the Earth's atmosphere

habitat surroundings that a particular species needs to survive. Habitats include coral reefs, grasslands, freshwater lakes, and deserts. Some creatures can live in more than one habitat.

incineration process of disposing of waste material by burning

incinerator device used to burn solid waste

industrialization process in which more and more emphasis is placed upon industry and manufacturing

leachate water that collects poisonous pollutants as it seeps through wastes, or polluted soil

leper someone or something that is isolated because of fears it will pollute others

malaria dangerous disease carried to humans by mosquitos

natural gas mixture of methane and other gases found underground or below the seabed which can be used as a fuel

nutrients nourishment

obsolete no longer in use, out of date

particulate tiny speck of solid matter in the air that is found in high concentrations in dust, smoke, and smog

pesticide poisonous substance which kills animal or insect pests

pollution waste products or heat which damage the environment in some way

radioactivity harmful rays and particles given off by certain substances as their atoms split

recovery (resource recovery) process of obtaining material or energy from materials which have been thrown away

recycling recovering waste material to make new products. Can also mean to reuse discarded products.

renewable energy energy from a source which can be restored and maintained. Wind and solar power are renewable energies.

resource natural thing found on Earth such as metals, trees, coal, or water, which can be used in some way

sanitary free from elements such as dirt or bacteria that can cause disease

sanitation safe collection and disposal of sewage and other waste

sediment small particles carried in liquid, such as silt in a river

sewage waste, usually including wastewater and human sewage

stagnant not moving or flowing

tetanus disease which can cause serious infection of a person's central nervous system and can lead to death

toxic waste waste that can produce injury if inhaled, swallowed, or absorbed through the skin

World Health Organization (WHO) international body, concerned with the health and well-being of the planet's population

Further reading

Books

Bowden, Rob. *Waste Recycling and Reuse* (Hodder Wayland, 2001)
This book examines the issues of rising levels of waste throughout
the world and the human, economic, and environmental costs of
the problem

Green, Jen. *Wasteful World* (Chrysalis Children's Books, 2004)
This is a book for children that looks at litter and household waste and
what impact it can have on the environment.

Morgan, Sally. *Waste Disposal* (Franklin Watts, 2000)
Part of the Earth Watch series, this title explains the basic issues around
the major types of wastes and how different materials are recycled.

Parker, Steve. *Green Files: Waste and Recycling* (Heinemann, 2003)
This relatively short account of the issues surrounding waste and recycling
is easy to understand.

Parker, Steve. *Protecting Our Planet: Waste, Recycling and Reuse*
(Wayland, 1997)
This is a general guide to the various forms of waste generated by human
activity, with material on potential solutions to the problem.

Tesar, Jenny. *The Waste Crisis* (Facts on File, 1995)
This title looks at the many forms of waste and the technologies used to
handle and dispose of it.

Websites

US Environmental Protection Agency
http://www.epa.gov/students/index.html
This is a large collection of webpages on environmental issues, including air and water quality, and pollution.

The Recycling Consortium
http://www.recyclingconsortium.org.uk/news/
Here you can find factsheets on a variety of waste topics including composting, landfills, and incinerators.

Addresses

Australian Conservation Foundation – ACF
340 Gore Street
Fitzroy
Victoria 3065
Australia
Tel: 61 2 92416265

Earth Policy Institute
1350 Connecticut Avenue, NW
Suite 403
Washington D.C., 20036
USA
Tel: (202) 496-9290

Friends of the Earth
26-28 Underwood Street
London
N1 7JQ
UK
Tel: 020 7490 1555

INDEX